CONCILIUM

Religion in the Eighties

CONCILIUM

Editorial Directors

Giuseppe Alberigo	Bologna	Italy
Gregory Baum	Toronto	Canada
Leonardo Boff	Petrópolis	Brazil
Antoine van den Boogaard	Nijmegen	The Netherlands
Paul Brand	Ankeveen	The Netherlands
Marie-Dominique Chenu O.P.	Paris	France
John Coleman S.J.	Berkeley, Ca.	U.S.A.
Mary Collins O.S.B.	Washington	U.S.A.
Yves Congar O.P.	Paris	France
Mariasusai Dhavamony S.J.	Rome	Italy
Christian Duquoc O.P.	Lyon	France
Virgil Elizondo	San Antonio, Texas	U.S.A.
Casiano Floristán	Madrid	Spain
Claude Geffré O.P.	Paris	France
Norbert Greinacher	Tübingen	West Germany
Gustavo Gutiérrez	Lima	Peru
Peter Huizing S.J.	Nijmegen	The Netherlands
Bas van Iersel S.M.M.	Nijmegen	The Netherlands
Jean-Pierre Jossua O.P.	Paris	France
Hans Küng	Tübingen	West Germany
Nicholas Lash	Cambridge	Great Britain
René Laurentin	Paris	France
Johannes-Baptist Metz	Münster	West Germany
Dietmar Mieth	Düdingen	Switzerland
Jürgen Moltmann	Tübingen	West Germany
Roland Murphy O.Carm.	Durham, N.C.	U.S.A.
Jacques Pohier O.P.	Paris	France
David Power O.M.I.	Washington, D.C.	U.S.A.
Karl Rahner S.J.	Munich	West Germany
Luigi Sartori	Padua	Italy
Edward Schillebeeckx O.P.	Nijmegen	The Netherlands
Elisabeth Schüssler Fiorenza	Hyattsville, Ind.	U.S.A.
David Tracy	Chicago	U.S.A.
Knut Walf	Nijmegen	The Netherlands
Anton Weiler	Nijmegen	The Netherlands
John Zizioulas	Glasgow	Great Britain

Lay Specialist Advisers

José Luis Aranguren	Madrid/Santa Barbara, Ca.	Spain/U.S.A.
Luciano Caglioti	Rome	Italy
August Wilhelm von Eiff	Bonn	West Germany
Paulo Freire	Perdizes-São Paulo	Brazil
Harald Weinrich	Munich	West Germany

Concilium 148 (8/1981): Ecumenism